INFORMATION
EXPLORER
JUNIOR

Learning and Sharing with a Wiki

by Ann Truesdell

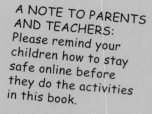

A NOTE TO PARENTS AND TEACHERS: Please remind your children how to stay safe online before they do the activities in this book.

CHERRY LAKE
Publishing

A NOTE TO KIDS: Always remember your safety comes first!

Published in the United States of America
by Cherry Lake Publishing
Ann Arbor, Michigan
www.cherrylakepublishing.com

Content Adviser: Gail Dickinson, PhD, Associate Professor, Old Dominion University, Norfolk, Virginia
Photo Credits: Cover, ©iStockphoto.com/fstop123; page 5, ©Andres Rodriguez/Dreamstime.com; page 7, ©SergiyN/Shutterstock, Inc.; page 9, ©Monkey Business Images/Shutterstock, Inc.; page 10, ©Gladskikh Tatiana/Shutterstock, Inc.; page 13, © Rob Marmion/Shutterstock, Inc.; page 15, ©Dmitriy Shironosov/Dreamstime.com; page 19, ©Greenland/Dreamstime.com; page 20, ©Jaimie Duplass/Shutterstock, Inc.

Library of Congress Cataloging-in-Publication Data
Truesdell, Ann.
  Learning and sharing with a wiki / by Ann Truesdell.
     pages cm. — (Information explorer junior)
  Audience: K to grade 3.
  Includes bibliographical references and index.
  ISBN 978-1-62431-132-1 (library binding) — ISBN 978-1-62431-264-9 (paperback) — ISBN 978-1-62431-198-7 (e-book) 1. Wikis (Computer science)—Juvenile literature. I. Title.

  TK5105.8882.T76 2013
  006.7'54—dc23   2013008589

Cherry Lake Publishing would like to acknowledge the work of The Partnership for 21st Century Skills. Please visit www.p21.org for more information.

Printed in the United States of America
Corporate Graphics Inc.
July 2013
CLFA13

Table of Contents

CHAPTER ONE

What Is a Wiki?

There are many different kinds of Web sites on the Internet. Some Web sites are for playing games or shopping. Others are helpful when you need to gather information. You probably have a few favorite Web sites that you check to read or watch updates about sports, music, or video games.

Did you know that there are also Web sites where you can add your own information that people see when they visit? These special Web sites are called **wikis**. Wikis are Web sites that many different people can **edit**, or change. One person creates a new page. Another person might come along and add some more facts. Another person could

When you visit a wiki, you might be seeing the work of dozens of people who have worked together.

add pictures or videos. Someone else may notice that a fact is wrong and change it to make the information correct. People work together to make wikis. This makes wikis great for schools. When we work together, we can learn a lot!

To get a copy of this activity, visit www.cherrylakepublishing.com/activities.

Try This

Wikis are very popular on the Web. See if you can find a wiki that has been created by students your age. Type "classroom wiki" into a search engine. You might have to click through a couple of pages of results to find the kind of examples you're looking for. Browse through three different wikis. Compare them to other Web sites that you have visited. What do you notice about wikis? How are they different from other Web sites? How are they alike?

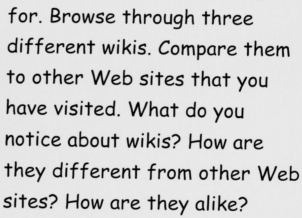

CHAPTER TWO

Why Use a Wiki?

You can use a wiki anywhere you can go online. This means that you can post on a wiki from school or from home. Other people on the Internet can view your wiki, too! This is what makes wikis such powerful sharing tools.

You can even use wikis from a smartphone or a tablet.

Wikis are great for group projects. They make it easier to create something as a group because everyone can add and edit wiki pages. Group members can edit pages from home or school. This means you don't even have to be in the same place as your fellow group members to get your project done. Everyone can add their thoughts, pictures, videos, and links to other Web sites. This means everyone gets a chance to share what

Your group members can work together from all around town!

Your teacher can show you how to access your class wiki.

he or she knows. If someone posts a fact that is incorrect, another group member can fix the mistake.

You can also use a wiki to share your work with others so that you can get **feedback**. Feedback is when someone offers you comments on your work. This is different

You can use a wiki's discussion board to send and receive feedback just as you would in person.

from just changing someone else's work. People giving feedback might tell you what they liked about your work or how you could make it better. Wikis usually have a special place on each page for people to give feedback and post comments. This feature is called the **discussion board**.

To get a copy of this activity, visit www.cherrylakepublishing.com/activities.

Try This

Wikis are all about sharing the information we know with others. Let's practice sharing, adding, and changing information by using a sheet of paper.

1. Get in a group with one or two other students.
2. Decide on a topic that everyone in your group knows about. You might choose a sport, television show, or animal.
3. Ask each person to think of some facts that they know about the topic.
4. Have the first group member write down a couple of facts or draw a picture about the topic.

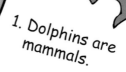

1. Dolphins are mammals.

5. Pass the paper to the next group member. This person can add new facts about the topic. He or she can also change things that the first group member wrote or drew, if it makes the wiki better.

6. Continue passing the paper around until everyone has added information.

1. Dolphins are mammals.
2. Dolphins are very intelligent.

Did your group members teach you anything new? Were you surprised by any changes that were made? What did you like and dislike about working on this paper wiki? Working together is not always easy, but it's fun to see how much we know when we put our minds together!

CHAPTER THREE

Working on Wikis

You can visit a wiki using your favorite Internet browser.

You can access a wiki the same way that you access any other Web site. Every Web site has its own **URL**, or address. If your teacher makes a wiki for your class, he or she will give you the URL to type into your Internet browser. That URL will take you to the wiki! You may also need to sign in using a username and password before you can edit the wiki. This makes it so that only certain people can change things on the wiki. For example, your teacher might want to share your work on the wiki with the whole world. But he or she might want only the kids in your class to be able to edit the wiki. That means that only you and your classmates will have usernames and passwords. Other visitors can see your work, but they cannot edit your pages.

You will need a URL, a username, and a password to log into your wiki.

URL: www.msjohnsonclasswiki.com

Username: MissJohnsonClassWiki

Password: DolphinWiki14

Take a moment to learn your way around your wiki before you dive in and start making changes.

When you first visit the wiki, take a good look at the first page and try to find your way around. Most wikis are more than one page. There will be links to other pages on the wiki, just like on most Web sites you visit. Your teacher might have different links for different school subjects. On some class wikis, each student has his or her own page. Other wikis have different pages for each group's project. Check out your class wiki to see how it is organized.

Each wiki page should have its own Edit button. Click this button to edit the page. Now you will be able to add your words to the page, delete parts of it, or change things that are already on it.

A **toolbar** might show up after you click the Edit button. The toolbar has many buttons that help you change other things on the page. For example, the toolbar might have a button that lets you change the colors on the page. The toolbar might also let you add links to other Web sites, pictures, videos, or files from your computer.

Finally, there will be another very important button on your page—the Save button! Be sure to click it when you are done editing so that your work will be posted online.

EDIT SAVE

To get a copy of this activity, visit www.cherrylakepublishing.com/activities.

Try This

Go back to one of the class wikis that you found in the activity in chapter 1. Or, if you have your own class wiki, go there! It's time to take a closer look at what makes a wiki special. See if you can find the following:

- how to log in
- different pages on the wiki
- a place to leave a comment, such as a discussion board
- the Edit button
- a toolbar for editing
- how to change **font** size and color
- how to add a picture to a page
- how to save a page

DISCUSSION BOARD

Don't make any changes that don't make the wiki better! Remember, you are just exploring right now. The time to make changes and add information will come soon!

CHAPTER FOUR

Following the Rules

Working on a wiki means working with other people. There are three very important rules that you should follow when you work on a wiki. These are rules that you should follow when you work face-to-face, too!

The first rule is to always be kind. When you change someone else's work or give them feedback, be careful that your words do not hurt anyone's feelings. Reread what you wrote to make sure it's something that you would say in person, too. You want to make changes that make your wiki better. If something on the wiki is wrong, you should change it. However, you should always make changes in a way that does not insult anyone.

Second, don't steal other people's work.

If you post information from a book on your wiki, be sure to give credit to the original author.

If you want to include information from another Web site, put it in your own words. You should also explain where you got your information. This can be as simple as adding a link to a Web site or adding the author and title of a book after you type out a fact.

Finally, be safe. Do not give out any information about yourself that you wouldn't want a stranger to know. Do not post your full name or address online. Remember that anyone can see what you have posted. If you are not sure about something, always ask a trusted adult.

Does your teacher have a class wiki for you to use? Do you have a wiki of your own? It's time for you to share what you know— and learn from others, too!

What will you do with your wiki?

To get a copy of this activity, visit www.cherrylakepublishing.com/activities.

Try This

Let's pretend that one of your classmates has posted the following information to your project page about oceans: *Oceans cover more than 70 percent of the earth's surface. The ocean water is divided up into four oceans: the Pacific, Atlantic, Antarctic, and Indian Oceans. The Atlantic Ocean is the largest. There are many different animals in these oceans.*

You are pretty sure that some of these facts are incorrect. Look in an encyclopedia under the topic "oceans" to double-check. How can you change the incorrect facts in a way that doesn't make your partner feel hurt or silly? Are there any facts that you could add to your group report? What images might you add to this page?

Always be kind when you make a comment.

Glossary

discussion board (dis-KUHSH-uhn BORD) a feature on many wikis that lets users send one another messages about the wiki; many wikis have a separate discussion board for each page in the wiki

edit (ED-ut) to correct or change something

feedback (FEED-bak) written or spoken reactions to something that you are doing

font (FAHNT) a style of text

toolbar (TOOL-bar) a menu bar that appears when editing a wiki page

URL (YOO AR EL) stands for Uniform Resource Locator, another way of saying Web address

wikis (WIH-keez) Web sites that allow multiple users to edit their pages

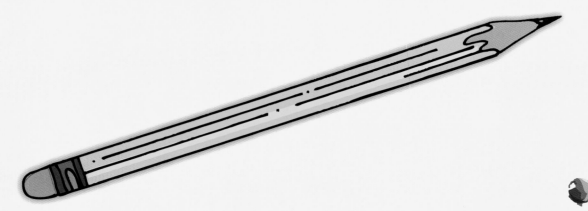

Find Out More

BOOKS

Fontichiaro, Kristin. *Getting Around Online*. Ann Arbor, MI: Cherry Lake Publishing, 2012.

Roslund, Samantha. *Join Forces: Teaming Up Online*. Ann Arbor, MI: Cherry Lake Publishing, 2013.

Truesdell, Ann. *Get to the Right Site*. Ann Arbor, MI: Cherry Lake Publishing, 2012.

WEB SITES

Wikipedia

www.wikipedia.org

Visit the biggest wiki on the Internet for information on almost any topic you can imagine.

Wikispaces

www.wikispaces.com

This site allows schools, teachers, and students to create their own educational wikis.

Index

About the Author

Ann Truesdell is a school library media specialist and teacher in Michigan. She and her husband, Mike, love traveling and spending time with their children, James, Charlotte, and Matilda.